HOW TO GET WHAT YOU WANT FROM A MAN

DARRELL CANTY

HOW TO GET WHAT YOU WANT FROM A MAN

iUniverse books may be ordered through booksellers or by contacting:

iUniverse
1663 Liberty Drive
Bloomington, IN 47403
www.iuniverse.com
844-349-9409

ISBN: 978-1-6632-3114-7 (sc)
ISBN: 978-1-6632-3115-4 (e)

Print information available on the last page.

iUniverse rev. date: 10/27/2021

CONTENTS

DEDICATION

I give a special dedication Pashawna Miller, Jameya Canty, Kei'ara Canty, Carlaya Canty, Aubriella Canty and Nayla Canty. I give a special thanks to all woman who has held down a good man. I give my allegiance and appreciation to all women who recognize the true value of a man. Also, I give a special dedication to all single mothers who has made it through life struggles with her head up and integrity in tack.

I also, dedicate this book to all the men who has weathered the storm with a woman not thinking, acting, and responding how God has intended her to. Responding to life's challenges with messy, disruptive, irrational, and even violet behavior. And their only response is I'm passionate about what I believe in.

ACKNOWLEDGEMENTS

I believe all women are design to want and receive as their natural state of being. I believe men are designed to give and provide to women, children, neighbors and our communities as their natural state of being. It is my intentions to deliver a strategy to fulfill the need to brings this ideal society together.

I give the utmost commitment, recognition and greater thanks to my Father God for everything to him I give all Credit.

PREFACE

I write this book because of my personal experience with a woman thinking, acting and receiving in her supreme being. I hope this book will help women understand their power, position and differences as a woman. More importantly I hope this book identify the issues with woman equality and clarify and explore the differences they represent.

I was raised in a two-parent home with much structure and an old school traditional upbringing. My first relationship I was a teenager, and like most teenagers I didn't know anything. As most men and young teenagers, they don't ask many questions and don't look for much help when it comes to relationships. I had the mindset of I will figure it out on my own. Until the internet naturally teenagers try to figure out things on their own, and that usually didn't work out. As I got older, I observed close around me and realized people didn't know how to act in their supreme being especially most women.

I only had two serious long-term relationships in my life. One for about thirteen years and the other for about nine years. The first relationship was like everyone else's. it was a good and normal relationship. The second relationship when I was with her, I realized I would do, give and provide almost anything within my means. Not only did I want to, it was easy to give to her. You may be asking can it be hard to give to a woman? Yes! So, I asked myself why? What was it that made me want to do for her, give too her and want the best for her? I wasn't sure if it was because of her or did I change somehow and became this great guy, No! I realized the way she was, it what I needed for me to be the way I was, and it seemed the way I was, it was what she needed for her to be the way she was. Although, we didn't agree with everything or have many commonalities we never got into an argument or harbored any animosity, not even misread each other's intentions. She never challenged me, used her words to harm me, tried to overpower me, control me, pressure me and she honored my wisdom. I never tried to control her, disrespect her, or disregarded her feelings. I cherished her and the way she gave of herself to me and to others. We never exchanged hurtful words or injured one another feelings the entire relationship. I would naturally give to her and give to her. This is when I knew a woman can get what she wants from a man. So, I began to evaluate and analyze her and myself to discover why. So here we go.

This book is inspired and driven to support and offer my daughters and granddaughters hope with an honest look at reality. Hopefully to give a clear reflection on how society tells them how they should behave and see themselves. Versus, how they truly should behave and see themselves with the best way to respond to life's challenges and get the best results. This book is for women with a desire to find their way back to true femininity, a genuine prospective of interpretation of a woman thinking, acting, and receiving in her supreme being. A true intent to provide useful and convincing information regarding todays woman and their power and position in life. For understanding and applying practical daily applications of acting and thinking like a lady while in her natural state. And at times how to act in opposition to her carnal nature while learning how to get what she wants from a man and still be liberated and full of self-importance. This information given does not offer nor represent anyone's claims or representation for everyone's situations. It's all based on the desires and discipline of a virtuous woman. I was moved by my personal experiences to deliver to women how to embrace their natural gifts and become the awesome woman they were created to be.

INTRODUCTION

Many women believe there is no one way to true womanhood. Many women also believe while in a relationship part of womanhood is to speak your mind and express the value of your thoughts. Although, a woman's expressed thoughts are valuable but does not represent her womanhood. My studies have discovered there is one way to true nature of womanhood, which is through self-respect, self-love and self-expression thru their femininity. Self-expression thru a woman's femininity meaning tactful and delicate. When a woman truly embraces these concepts along with becoming self-aware of one's behavior of treating herself with the right self-care, self-esteem and self-importance her womanhood is solid and her foundation is invaluable.

I will take you through the manipulated way most women today have been conditioned to think and act. I will reveal some of the fears of being alone, and why women are seeking after the "bad boy," and some of the pains of dealing with the millennial man. Also, revisiting the myth of God will send you a mate and why women shouldn't pursue a man. We'll even cover what a man and how a man is thinking and why you think he won't commit. I intend to deliver a clear picture or an ideal of why women won't get what they want from a man and how they can change that. I will deliver how a woman was designed to think and act to get the things she needs and want from a man.

The focus in society for many years of most women and the woman's movement has been for equality and opportunity. The woman's liberation has forgotten some of the great natural attributes of a woman given by God. One of the natural attributes of a woman are femininity, being feminine is not being weak or a disposition of lacking or less than, rather a unique ability of being delicate and tactful while identifying herself separate from a man (appearance, nurturing and vulnerable). Another natural attribute is being a helpmate, being a helpmate is not one who is in a position of need or co-dependent, rather one who guide, assist and cultivates for a better outcome for all involved. I believe the best natural attribute of a woman and my favorite is being charitable, one who gives of herself and her resources sincerely. A woman in her true position is priceless! These natural attributes will reveal an ideal of how a woman can get what she wants from a man.

This book was also created to understand the significance of a good woman's contributions. To reveal the importance to how a woman affects all relationship by her gifts or lack of. Also, how instrumental a woman's position is to our future in society. How the modern woman has significantly contributed to the downfall of our family structure today. I have been inspired to write this type of book and much needed for the western world. Not in any way to express a woman should go back to the way it was, but to understand a woman true power and position with self, her Creator, and a man. There is a demand for the many women who has rejected their natural place as an absolute lady and to return to her position. Women want what they want but don't know how to get it. Let me help a little…

Women need to know how and why they should stop contributing as the main cause of breakdown of the two-parent household, and some women thinking that having children is one way of getting what she wants from a man. I have heard, maybe thousands of times over the years how women don't need men and how they can be the man and woman of their family. This doesn't work. Let me help a little…

This book will also uncover how a woman can be a critical thinking, upstanding, independent and self-respecting lady. While still be feminine, a helpmate, charitable and respected by others. A true woman acting and thinking in her natural state will not compete with a man or another woman with her womanhood in any way, only to show herself set aside and unique by her own contributions. A woman with a mindset to compete with her man in any way automatically removes her from her natural state as well as the man.

This information will expand on what it means to be alone and the difference in being lonely. Also, guide you through the reality that everyone is not by design to be with someone. It's all about choices and free will. The plan is to give those with an open mindset an opportunity of regaining their natural state of acting like a woman and think like a lady and getting you what you want from a man. Let me hep a little...

CHAPTER 1
WHY WOMEN WANT THE WRONG GUY

A FALSE HOPE "THE BAD BOY"

The woman's natural biological and psychological attraction to a man is his giving nature, masculinity and masculine disposition. No matter how independent, her upbringing, and strong a woman is her natural attractions is the masculinity and authoritative nature in a man. And that's why women gravitate toward the "bad boy." The "bad boy" image gives women the desire behind the mysterious and adventures masculine disposition of a bad boy. This attraction applies to the traditional woman as well as the millennial woman. The media portrays the masculinity in the bad boy that makes him so desirable. Most women may believe the bad boy can protect her in any situation, he's so adventurous and he fears nothing. I believe most women are attracted to the wild side and mystery in a man "bad boy" because they seem to be somewhat unavailable. I believe that it is something in the DNA of women that resonates within their emotions and drives them to curiosity, mystery, challenge and that chase in life. As well as their natural need to want to be conquered. Women mostly see the excitement in the bad boy, and they want him to be the one. Some may think that most women don't gravitate to the "bad boy," I believe they all do but may not all act on it because of some form of fear. Many believe most women enjoy the chase to get the man and most men enjoys when they chase that "good girl" turned bad, But the truth is women just enjoy the chase. The chase can excite and entice a woman despite the particulars of the

1

man. Also, many women who pursue the "bad boy" don't have to worry about being that "good girl." This relieves the pressures of the woman needing to be good or to be a certain way because they know the "bad boy" type is not concerned with finding a good or bad girl.

The media also plays a big part in making the "bad boy" so attractive to a woman with so much eye-catching drama in the media. The media can play so many undertones that makes the "bad boy" look so good. He is so tuff, so cool, he knows what to say, what to do and he's what every woman wants and so mysterious. Women may be thinking If I get with that bad boy, he will bring so much adventure to my life. I believe that all women want some level of adventure in their life, and many believe that the "bad boy" will continue to bring that to them, over and over again.

Many women are so busy consciously and subconsciously taking on projects that entertaining the very challenge of a "bad boy" sound so exciting and forbidden. A lot of woman wants to be the one who changes the "bad boy" and pull that good guy out of him. Most "bad boys" are truly bad boys. One of the problems with a woman chasing a man is their natural structure is worrying. Women just naturally worry in life. A woman is not designed to chase a man and many times she may replace her worrying with control, and we know how controlling someone never work. Although many women may grow out of the "bad boy" phase I believe they will never truly appreciate the "nice guy." Never!

CHAPTER 2
GOD WILL NOT SEND YOUR MATE

I know, I know we've heard it time and time again. God will send me my soulmate; I wonder who hasn't heard this before? Most people were raised in or around some form of religion and some of them teaches people to believe that God will send you your soulmate. With this mindset some religious and non-religious people would believe that the one they are with is "the one" based off that. They may believe they have received divine confirmation from God or through other religious leaders, that they are with the one they supposed to be with.

Many women may believe the only reason God has not sent them their soulmate and they have been experiencing so much heartache is because they haven't put God first in their lives. Not!

Some women may believe they cannot experience the fullness of life as a single person as we should all be with someone to experience completeness. Not!

Some women may believe that they are less than, if they are not with someone who loves and cherish them. Not!

Some women may even believe they have that right, If God is just, He will send me a mate. You may believe that God will put you in a relationship. If God puts people together in relationship, why do so many relationships fail? If God know the end before the beginning and is Alpha and Omega and knows us down to the strands of hair on our head, wouldn't he choose our mates better, right? If God is all knowing and all wise why does he fail with matching up his own creation?

All these concepts may seem very appealing, yet it all contradicts God's word. God made us in his image *alike free will.* God made us in his image; mind, Free will and with emotion. God loves us and choose us freely, not by force, just as he invites us to love and chose freely. A person doesn't truly love unless he or she can choose the option.

So, simply put, God will not choose your mate. Again, God will not choose your mate. Again, God will not choose your mate. God is not going to choose you a mate, and not choose your salvation. Right! Many women may still believe today that God has assigned a husband for them. You may say my marriage is ordained; it is ordained not because he invited you it's because you invited him. Some may think their marriage is divine and the ones who don't believe is not. Where is that written. Many may believe that God has said this in the bible, but it is not so. God made us in his image which includes the main course *free will,* this mean God cannot choose for you or he will go against his own word. "God's word says in Proverbs 18:22, *"He who finds a wife finds a good thing and obtains favor from the Lord."* That means the man must find (pursue) you. This doesn't mean that God has a husband prepared for ever woman seeking marriage, nope. I believe this verse is directed primarily for the man, because of a man's nature. Since He created us, He knows us. A man who is not focus and committed to one woman will always be seeking women. Therefore, I believe He (a man) who finds a wife obtains favor from the Lord. Men must act in opposition to his carnal nature in order to seek one woman. So, women stop waiting for your soulmate and start learning how to choose the right man when he chooses you. To a woman this should mean if you prefer to be found by a man to make you his wife is to prepare yourself to be a wife. Become valuable as a wife, available to be a wife and prepared for a man to wife you. Make it difficult for any man not to want to make you his wife. One more time, if you prefer to be found by a man to make you his wife is to prepare yourself to be available and valuable to a man. This mean to prepare yourself to display your femininity. Feminine, show yourself to be delicate and tactful with your words and actions. show yourself separate from a man with your appearance and your nurturing ways.

Be unique in who you are and sensitive with your interactions with him (the one you choose). If you could only be kind, loving, caring, giving etc.... to anyone on earth let it be with the one you chose to spend your life with. Also show him you are a helpmate by learning how to aid and assist him with his daily dealings and putting your vision within his vision. Also, let him see how charitable you are with who you are and willing to share you and your possessions. Be feminine delicate, a helpmate assist, and being charitable is part of your natural gift to a man and our community at large. Stop listening to women especially those who don't have a man or can't keep a man and don't know a man telling you otherwise. This is another reason why a woman shouldn't pursue a man.

CHAPTER 3
WOMEN DON'T PURSUE MEN

Today it is common to have a woman approach a man. Many people believe it is not only OK but may be needed depending on their circumstances. It's just the way of the world. Right! Some, relationship experts may give different technic on approaching a man. Many may say to approach a man make eye contact and add a smile, then let him know you're interested. Some may say just go up to man show him you're interested and start flirting say or do something to get him interested in you. It's not the old school in me that say's this is not the best way to start or engage a relationship it's the research student in me saying based on the nature of a man, not so good. If you are just trying to hook up and that's your goal ok, but not the best for building a relationship. Although many millennial men think this behavior is acceptable because they are millennial men. The problem with this is the millennial man is lacking many of the essentials all women need today. Like wanting to be the main provider, his giving nature, masculinity and having a masculine disposition in the relationship.

Now I'm not against a woman trying to get a man to approach her because that makes a huge difference. There are many things you can do to encourage this. Always look and act your best. Pay attention to your tone, facial expressions, and body language. Always carry your smile and use your smile often. Develop and be aware of your communicating skills. It's important to understand and be aware of your emotions and how you respond to people and situations. Practice things daily that make you feel good about yourself because it shows and attracts people (men).

A woman shouldn't pursue or chase a man in any way, because it is by natural design. By natural design men are the hunters and the woman are the prey. The natural design is a man needs to be ready and willing to hunt while attracted to what he is hunting. A man needs to desire a woman's attitude, femininity, physique and the way she gives herself to him. This is because this facilitates a man's masculine disposition and frames the relationship. Our creator designed a man's nature to always chase after a woman by his eyes through his attraction, how thoughtful she is and how gentle and soft she is toward him. Just because many men have adapted to the ruff, unkind, verbal combative, and hard as a man deminer doesn't mean this is what men want. When a woman is acting delicate and tactful while identifying herself separate from a man through her appearance, nurturing and vulnerability. For this reason, you see men in their sixties, seventies and eighties still chasing after a woman. In the Bible the word shall cleave, or cling means in English to glue, to adhere, to stick and to join. The Hebrew word shall cleave, or cling expands more on its meaning like, to adhere, to abide, to fast together, and to follow. The Hebrew meaning is more expressive and broader in its meaning. The Hebrew meaning to adhere is to stay and observe, to abide is to stand for and bear with, to fast together is to go together and to follow means to pursue and chase after. So, a man is to cling to his woman, stay and observe, abide in and stand for his woman; continue to pursue and chase after her. The Bible say's for this reason a man shall cleave not the woman shall cleave. Even after a man is married or has caught the woman, if she no longer remains chaseable a man become disinterested because of his natural instinct to pursue after. Most men stop the chasing after he has the woman, because the woman no longer does, say and present herself to be chaseable. A man is the pursuer by nature.

Again, for this reason, a man was design to pursue a woman and not a woman to pursue a man.

There are other reasons why woman should not pursue a man. A woman needs to be cherished, needs affection, and personal devotion. These types of needs a man must want to deliver because he chases after a woman and only when he is pursuing. If the woman is the pursuer the man has no drive or need to cherish her. Why? Because she's chasing him, giving to him, try to pressure him and following him with heaviness she will lose as a result. He's good! Cherish who? What affection, she's after me? Devotion time is when she catches me, then she will get her personal devotion. A man will truly demonstrate these behaviors when he is pursuing a woman. A woman gets these things by being chased and chaseable. When a woman is and show herself to be valuable threw her femininity, a helping nature and charitable, a man will pursue. If a woman chases a man it will be difficult for him to see value in her because she is out of her natural state, and most likely won't work. A man needs to want to spend time and be with his woman or it won't work. Even if a woman is whole, self-aware and prepared it doesn't mean a woman should pursue a man, at all. Because if a woman pursues a man who isn't pursuing her, she will make it hard for him to ever be hers. Why, the first thing that a man needs to accept about accepting a woman is he believes it's his choice and he's ready. So, when a man is pursuing a woman, he either believes he is ready, or he knows he is ready for that woman.

If a woman is chasing after a man, he may not trust why the woman is chasing him or believe the woman's intension aren't in his best interest. He won't be yours, even if he commits. If a man is self-aware and ready, and he wants you he will be pursuing you, so stop. If there are no men pursuing you it's not the men, it's you. Although, some women need to accept that all men are not wanting or ready for a relationship. If a man say he is not ready, he is not ready, even if you think he is ready. Even if a man is not ready but thinks he is ready it may work, because he thinks he is ready. Many women may believe if a man says he is not ready he doesn't want to commit. Not wanting to commit and not ready doesn't mean the same. If a man doesn't want to commit, he will show you by his behavior, actions and most likely he will tell you. If a man gives in to a woman when he is not ready or believes he is not ready, or he did not choose you, he is truly not yours nor committed to you. Regardless if he is sleeping with you, living with you, sharing with you, he is certainly not yours, not yours, not yours. Only when a man chooses you, he is ready. Not when you say I'm not just dating for nothing we need to set a date. Or, we've been together two years now, either you marry me or I'm leaving. And he marries you. By a man accepting it by your pressures to be his, he is not yours. A man needs to be willing and ready to choose you. So, women, stop pursuing a man, stop trying to get him to commit, and prepare yourself to be available, valuable and rear. As a woman you should hope a good man finds you as a treasure, because you are self-aware, self-love, and emotionally rational. Just as a man should hope a woman finds him to be valuable as a protector and provider, self-aware, with self-love and hard to replace.

To pursue a man does not mean you lose the upper hand, or you should feel embarrassed. This doesn't mean you have less value because you're after him and he's not after you. To pursue a man doesn't mean you won't be adored or respected. This doesn't even mean you are not worth the fight. It's not about the man didn't have do any work to get you because you pursued him. Not even that you made it to so easy. It just means you are making it hard for that man to see the value in you. Valuable things are hard to get, obtain or require, that why people she value in them. What's hard to find is a woman that is kind, giving, patient and easy to get along with. I know you are working at a good job. You have your own money and place to live. You even have your own children. All you need is him; you say. Although, those things sound good, but they have much more value to you than to him. You can't find the right man for you; you can only accept it when the right man finds you. To pursue a man means you are not in your natural state which takes him out of his natural state.

A man needs to be the pursuer and attracted by a woman's attitude, nature and visual physique everything else is just a benefit to the man, if you are ready for him. Meaning the woman needs to have the right attitude, mannerism and physical attraction, for a man to chase a woman. One of the basic reasons a man is the one to pursue a woman is his desire for physical connection, I mean sex. Most women are not that interested in sex, or sex only. So, most women who are pursuing men are not out to give him what his basic needs or desires are, just what she wants. Women want what got them to sex from the man mostly and not just the sex. Therefore, a man needs to be the pursuer as he pursues a woman because he wants her. If a woman pursues a man it could be for many reasons like, she's lonely, she needs economic help, she needs moral or emotional support, or she is looking for a father figure for her children etc.... not just she wants him!

Because of the nature of the man there are only the three essential qualities of a woman needed for a man to chase after which are, a good attitude, show herself to be irresistible in her femininity and attractive. Irresistible in her femininity means he believes your actions show you are inviting, approachable, and only want him. This means there is nothing for a man to really do in order to chase. Just start chasing. The chase requires a woman to be in her nature state. For a woman to chase she needs to be out of her nature element. She needs to find things about the man, how much he makes, what type of car he drives, what type of work he does, does he have kids and so on. Or, maybe do some of the types of things he likes, or even do something to be notice by him. Therefore, it should be clear a woman needs to be herself just to be chased by a man and not the other way. Some woman may do many things to change their demeanor in order to chase after a man, to be a good fit it won't work. Some woman tries to add her education and financial status to her reasons to be chase by a man, it won't work. Some woman tries to align her likes or dislikes with the man in order to build an attraction, it won't work. Some woman tries to find areas in a man's life where he may need some compassion to gain some attraction. Even worst some women try to make changes in the man for her to chase after him. Stop! Be yourself and embrace your nature.

This doesn't mean a woman should not make herself available to meet the right man when he crosses her path. If a woman has found self-love, and knows what self-respect is, and is somewhat self-aware of her thoughts and behavior, yes make yourself available. If a woman is emotionally intelligent and understands the difference between the respect of a man and the respect of a woman, yes make yourself available. If a woman has control over her tongue and honors a man's decisions, yes make yourself available. If you are a woman who finds herself a helper, giver and increases the good with her friends, family and work, yes make yourself available. If a woman believes there is no time when she should ever tear down her man with her words, yes make yourself available. If a woman does these things, I am certain a man will pursue you. If not, you are not ready you shouldn't make yourself available until you are ready. Because you are not ready to be pursued. The only thing a man needs to do is be ready or believe he is ready, then chase and chase after the woman.

CHAPTER 4
WHY HE WONT COMMIT TO YOU?

Society has people involved in so many things and keeping us so busy many women may think it's never going to be the right time. Maybe because many of us are so involved in our social world and not so much involved in the real world he or she doesn't really see you as priority. Many of us are programed to react to whatever is going on in life instead of choosing our daily direction in life. With these types of life's pressures some women may think this is the reason he won't commit. These are not the reasons he won't commit.

We have too much information and too much we want to do. We live in a time where the quantity of information and entertainment we receive is overwhelming. The choices we face daily constantly influences us to stimulate our wants and desires. The sad news is we are under the media's manipulation of believing we need to be constantly busy and maybe there are women who believe this may be why your man won't commit. These are not the reasons he won't commit.

You really believe he loves you and so far, everything is going well, but he won't commit. You may think he's working a lot and just doesn't have the time for you. He keeps telling you that he needs to get his finances right to provide for you. You're just not sure. Maybe it was that time he told you he was badly hurt in a previous relationship. He did everything he thought he supposed to do and treated his ex-girl very well and it didn't work out. Just like he treats you very well. Maybe it's because he just got out of a serious relationship and he says he needs a break. Are any of these answers good enough why he won't commit? No. These are not the reasons he won't commit.

There may be many reasons, but the number one reason a man won't commit to a woman is the pressure a woman puts on him, to commit. Pressure, pressure and pressure. When a woman is consistently pressuring her man to commit it will cause him to do the opposite. This type of action many times will cause the man to have some resentment toward the woman. When this happen, the man will feel obligated not to commit and stay the course. Usually when someone believes they are not ready and feel reluctant to commit, they won't. another way of saying women don't pursue a man.

Sometimes the reason why he won't commit is he feels you are trying to change him. When a woman is trying to change a man, it's telling him he's not good enough for you. He's lacking ambition, consistency, there are so many things he's not doing right. Why would he commit? It is also telling him you are never going to be happy with him unless he changes. Why would he commit? The more someone try to change another person it will push them away, away from commitment. Another reason a man won't commit is he fears the consequences if he does commit. Men will usually weigh the pros and cons many times before he commits. It's all about if he believes he is gaining more than he is losing.

This may be the most important reason he won't commit; does he really trust you. There can be many questions in a man's mind when it comes to him committing. Do you want him to rescue you financially or emotionally? Do you make him feel you are desperately committed to being married by a certain date? Do you make him feel being married is more important than having a great relationship? Does he feel you are trying to control him and the direction of your relationship? He may be thinking these things if he doesn't trust your reason why you want to commit. I mean trust in a way that you truly are considering his interest and his benefit. If you really show him that you are concerned about what he wants as much as what you want, this is the best way to get a man to commit. This is the trickiest reason because many women fake like they are concerned about a man to get him to commit. It should be what is best for us instead of what is best for now. If he has pursued you and is clear about how he feels about relationships, he will commit.

Most men don't really see the benefits in marriage. Many times, the media and society at large show so many negative outlooks to men and marriage. Especially, when there are children involved and most of the time there are children involved. Many men see the financial commitment and the pitfalls in the many failed marriage in this country every year. Where it may show most of the time the man financial hardship behind a failed marriage. If the man doesn't see in advance a successful marriage, why commit.

Some of the ways you can help a man commit without the constant pressure is understanding his background. Try to understand how he see and value marriage. As well as understanding his views on money, sex, child rearing, and your current relationship. Is your current relationship healthy and happy, if not why commit? Most men just want to get along. Most women just want things to go her way. The key is finding out what is he thinking.

CHAPTER 5
WHAT IS A MAN THINKING?

IF HE IS GOOD TO YOU, IS HE GOOD FOR YOU?

Does he truly like you? Does he need to feel like you are perfect for him? What is he feeling? How can I be sure? Does he really want to commit? Does he trust me? Does he truly love me? What is he thinking?

Most women are constantly worrying many questions to be answered when they began and are in relationships. It may seem that he is really into you, but can you be sure. More importantly how can you tell if he is good for you regardless how good he is to you.

Men aren't cut off from their feelings and they have all the feeling as a woman. The difference is their feeling are not activated like a woman's feeling are with everything that happens. Also, men don't usually base their decisions of their feeling rather their logic. For example, a woman who believes a man who loves her she may feel he should give up his goal, desire, life etc. to blend in with hers.

A man may approach this differently. For example, if he believes a woman who loves him should consider if she fits in with his goals, desire, and his life and if it would be good to blend for both. But not give up her goals for his if it is not good for both.

He would consider is this practical to blend based on the facts and not the feelings.

Because most traditional guys don't tell you how he feels, and sometimes it may be difficult for him to express himself. It is important women to stop paying attention to everyone around and pay attention to him. Men usually express their feeling by their actions and show signs that they care about you. Sometimes it's the special way you guys interact with each other. It could be many things that remind him of you that he needs to tell others in a way that expresses joy and good times when he's with you. Because men are emotionally unexpressive and simple, it will be easy to show he's in a good mood when you're in his presence. When a man is into you, he will take efforts to make you smile and laugh. Most men that are into their woman want to help put their woman in a good mood. A man who is into you and not shamed of your behavior he will gladly introduce you to the people that is the closest to him in his life. **Your behavior is more important to him than your looks** when he introduce you to his friends and family. If a man is into you, he will ask your opinion if you respect him when he is making decisions because your input matters even if he doesn't use your input. Most men are not curious or curious about you so don't put a lot of concern about how he feels about you if he doesn't ask you a lot of questions about you and your day. Men only asked these types of questions in the beginning when he wants you to like him. Most men try their best to be a closed book when it comes to their feelings. So, whatever personal info he shares with you it means he likes and trust you. If you care for him do not ever use that information against him or share it with others. Because He won't ever forget it.

In the beginning it always easy for a man and woman to treat each other with kindness, care and passion. People are good to each other because of their chemistry and desires to connect in a physical way. So, we do thing to make the other person interested and happy. We say and do good thing for the other person to get them to like us and want us. Simply we all want to feel good and we enjoy when other people cause us to feel this way. Because of this many women are so concerned with how a man makes her feel. Sometime a person can put so much interest on how the person treats them they lose focus on if he or she is good for them. Men and women can treat each other with acts of kindness and do nice things and not be good for that person. Many women focus so much on the man being good to her, when it more important in a healthy relationship to be good for each other even when there are times you are not good to each other. It's easy to treat people good in the beginning of a relationship because there is no negative thoughts, regrets or negative experiences with that person. Many women believe they just want someone to treat them fairly and equitably with and ongoing romance burning in their lives. When in fact it is more important for someone to be good for us because of who they are and not because who we are, or what we do for them.

If a man believes it's not his responsibility to be the primary provider in the relationship, he is not good for you, regardless who makes what. This doesn't mean he needs to make the most money, this mean he takes on the responsibility of making sure that you guys are financially secure. A man thinking as a provider is always focused on contributing to the foundation of the family. Providing a spiritual, financial and emotionally healthy environment is a man's true nature. This is his responsibility rather the woman is working or not. So, this man needs to be able to lead the family regardless of the pressured by his woman. If a man does not believe this, he is not ready, if you don't believe this, you're not ready. If a man believes that you should be equally financially, spiritually, or emotionally responsible for everything, he is not good for you. A man will never be equally emotional to a woman even if the woman is emotional intelligent.

Men and women aren't affected the same. A man in a relationship needs to lead in these areas regardless. This doesn't mean a woman can't contribute, guide or even make more money than the man, she can be more spiritually grounded than the man or she is in control of her emotional behavior more than the man. The man needs to know he's supposed to be the one responsible, managing and leading the family in this position. Not equal partners. Why? A man nature is not to worry like a woman's nature. When it comes to financial issues. Why? A man nature is not to constantly question his spiritual challenges. Why? A man nature is not to lead by his emotions rather the information and conditions given. As a man, by providing the financial stability and a solid emotional foundation it allows a woman to be comfortable and charitable of herself. If a man doesn't believe he needs to add and improve on his woman and family, he is not good for you or the family. These are some of the things most men are and should be thinking.

A man that is good for you has certain standards. Most men think a woman needs relational compassion and emotional intimacy from a man that puts her needs before his own. Most men think this even many of the millennial men. Most men think he needs to know the truth about himself and is clear of his thinking. Most men think he needs to be aware of his strength and weakness in order to lead. Most men are aware and thinks he needs to know what he needs to be managed in his life and how. Most men think they can't respond on how he feels when things get bad only to the situation for the best outcome. Most men think by being honest with you and open with you and knows how to make you feel will help you fully be comfortable with him. Find a man who has been single long enough to think he needs to be the practical one in the relationship with dealing in life challenges. Not that a woman can't it's just easier for a man. The most important thing you need know what a man is thinking is he thinks a strong foundation of treating himself in a healthy spiritual, emotional and Psychological way is most important thing in a relationship. Because this will determine how he will treat you as well. Most men think they need to love themself enough to set high standards and set good principles. Most men think they need to be the one who establishes a foundation of providing, protecting and cultivating his environment. This man will have everything he needs to love, support and treat you well. This is a man good for you and will be good to you. Any man thinking if he can't add to and improve his woman life, is not ready for you. Although, this may not be most millennial men thinking. Be careful with dealing with the millennial man.

CHAPTER 6
WOMEN LIBERATION & MEN DISPLACEMENT

Most women found their place after the woman's liberation, and most men lost their place in civilization after the woman's liberation. When this happened, the nation shifted slowly but significantly in the western world. I believe this may have been one of the most significant movement in all of mankind's history. This movement has affected migration, education, politics, technology, economics, individualism basically every facet of our society. Women liberation originally and primary was for the fight for equality in the workforce and equal political participation. This movement was necessary for women. No one should get paid less for doing the same job because of the race, age, or sexual orientation. No one should be denied the right to vote or participate in political affairs because of the race, age or sexual orientation. And more importantly no one should be treated less than because of their race, age or sexual orientation.

Since then there have been multiple women liberation movements. This followed the elimination of women feminist model, and began women equal to a man, and women freedom from a man "women don't need men." But the most powerful movement has been the woman's sexuality movement. Women sexuality is no longer subject to or for the procreation and since of duty to have sex on the woman's part in any relationship including marriage.

WOMEN SEXUALITY MOVEMENT

Let's start with sexuality and move back up to the elimination of the women feminist model. Women has created and demanded "desire" as the worth and value in a relationship and without the condition of sex, domestic duties, and a partner commitment as responsibility or duty. Except for the past sixty years or so in this country sex use to be for procreation, a momentary fulfillment of satisfaction and a since of duty on the part of the woman. This is because women don't want sex like men, they want what got them to sex. There has never been a since of duty for a man because the nature of a man needs sex, without the necessity any other surrounding desire. Another key factor is contraception and its impact for women has helped liberated them from the conventional role as a woman in a relationship. Now I'm not saying a woman should have the first and last say so on procreation, I'm all for it. But we're just talking about the act of sex, not the aftertaste. Because of the new demand of desire on relationships it has created not only liberation but a new separation.

Now sexuality is part of our culture that represent our identity, pleasures, connection and desires. Sexuality is at the forefront of commencing almost all intimate relationships. This is credited to the Women's movement of sexuality. Sexuality today is now rooted in desire and no more in commitment, duty and role of a man and woman.

The condition of having sex for women today is all based on desires. Most sexual desires are based on the connection, possibilities or potentials with a woman's romantic experience on how she feels about the sexual encounter that lead her to the act. Or how she feels at the moment. Not the act itself. Meaning most women desires are not based on the sex itself rather how she feels on what connects her to the experience. Or what has disconnected her at the moment. For example, it could be the challenge, it could be the mystery, it could be the playfulness, it could be the uniqueness, or it could be his edge. Just like a woman's lack of desire could be the reason not to have sex, he doesn't help with the children, he doesn't make enough money, he didn't take out the trash, he doesn't make me feel special, or any unfulfillment she is feeling.

Most women are not interested in just sex, only. Women turn themselves on and off because of these things. Because the act of sex is based on desires for a woman everything or anything can affect her desires. Men have been and still are motivated by motivation by their eyes that attraction them to woman that leads straight to sex. A woman's attitude toward him and her femininity is extra. For men, this has been the same since the beginning of time. Since a woman no longer need to feel obligated to a man to have sex and only when she desires it, most men don't know how to deal with, and some can't measure up? So, the man becomes displaced.

WOMEN FEMININE THEORY

This theory focus has been primarily on gender inequality with political and legal rights. The original feminist system was designed to benefit men from women subordination. This movement has been prejudiced on cultural differences rather than genetic or natural reasons. Although, femininity is no longer considered a set of behaviors, mannerism or natural physique it is more compared to social impacts and social status. Many may not understand or agree but true feminist is derived from a person nature, natural state and a way of being delicate and tactful behavior. Feminine is not based on gender, gender is based on the interpretation or human sex differences as biological, and this theory support reasons of intellectual or progressive, rather than a way of being delicate and tactful. It seems that women have walked away from the benefits of being feminine that has caused many men confusion and separation. This has caused many women to become displaced of their true position.

WOMEN DON'T NEED MEN

Way… back when before the 1970's America had a picture of the traditional roles of men, women and family that everyone understood. There were cultural roles for the man and woman. The roles of the woman would be home making, raising the children and tending to her husband. The role of the man would be earning the money to provide and protect the home, provide food, shelter and clothing and all the necessities of life. These types of roles required the need for the man and the need of the woman. These roles also defined what described a man and what described a woman which made understanding relationship and family easy. Most household in the country at this time men and women had mutual respect of one another because of their roles. These roles also identified and was recognized how their love of each other was expressed. Since world war II the woman had to go out to work. So, when the man came back from the war, he found himself without a job. Because most of the jobs in that day was factory jobs and most of the factory jobs were occupied by the woman. Now there is no woman in the home tending to the house, children and her man and the man is without a job. This moment in time shifted everything for relationships, family's social connections, education, politics, economics, especially how women no longer need a man.

Now-a-days many men don't know how to be a man, because our past time use to define what is a man was simple, he provided, protected, give her children, groceries, car, etc.… and cultivate what was his. Since then no one has told a man his new position as a man or how to function in this new world. Today the average man meets the average woman, she has her own house so, the man can't offer her that. The average woman today has her own car so, he can't offer her that. The average woman today over the age of twenty has children so he can't offer her that. The average woman today over the age of thirty either has a college degree or two, or she is earning more money than the average man in her age group so, his money she really doesn't need. So, the media tells her she doesn't need a man and she show the man she no longer needs him, and the man becomes displaced.

Women are not designed to want a man, rather to need a man when it comes to emotional and physical security, stability, necessity and resources. It all has changed! Especially, since many women no longer believes she needs a man.

WOMEN EQUAL TO A MAN

As I mention before women liberation originally and primary was for the fight for equality in the workforce, civil and political rights. This movement has evolved from getting the same pay and being treated fairly in the political area, and a person. To I can do and be whatever a man can do and be. This has spread throughout sports, education, politics, technology, economics, and every industry in the country. I'm not mad, but what do I tell the men? And most areas women are doing it better, longer and continually elevating the game for men to compete with them even inside the house. Again, what do I tell the men? I have discovered it is natural for a man to compete with another man rather win or fail is easily received. It is not natural for a man's psychological state to compete with a woman especially in the household because it will eventually affect both of their mental wellbeing. Because of the friction and conflict, it will cause. All men are driven to pursue a woman, just because the man's nature. Unless his upbringing was not natural. Basically, if a man is not in pursuit of a woman or his plans does not include the gain of a woman or women, he may feel undervalued, regardless of his financial status. Even with the pursuit for men with women today many men feel they are not confident enough and so, the man becomes displaced.

THE DISPLACEMENT OF MEN

Before the women's liberation the mainstream of society set the rules and expectations of the man, woman, family and community. People's identity was determined by society's and the community in which their position, stability and respect was viewed and not oneself. The old society mainly produced a community of what people do. Now the new social society produces a people of who I am or who I am going to be. A happy healthy life before the liberation for many has been having a good job, home, being healthy and plenty of food to eat. Today's happy healthy life could include many things. Many may consider things like, having an intimate relationship with a partner and love ones, having a good best friend, traveling, facilitating good work relationships, economic advancement etc....

Between the women's movement and the new millennial man most men just don't seem to know who or what they supposed to be or do. The women movements have been so powerful and quietly victorious many men are still walking around holding their head, wondering why, why, why... Since the beginning of time the man's role have been the protector, provider and cultivator, but now it's much more than that. Since the woman role no longer exist this has change how men and women relate. Since men still want to have sex with women and women no longer has a duty to have sex with her mate. This new system or way of life has demanded men to learn romance, develop excitement, and continue to create the next new thrill, men must adjust. Men naturally haven't been drawn to participate and express feelings. Men have never been taught to be aware of a sharing with a woman's feeling. Although, most women expect this. The new man needs to become more aware of how to deal with women emotions past misfortune, heartbreak or tragedy. Other than the old traditional things like, complement his woman, bring her flowers, and provide her with gifts, and hold her when it's needed, that's not enough. The new man is expected to be romantic, attractive, passionate, adventurous and endearing along with maintaining his traditional role provide, protect and cultivate. The new man is expected to cook and clean along with the other domestic duties of a home. The new man is expected to adhere to the new mom role of tending to babies and help developing small children. The new man is to be a co-parent and nurturing to the children. The new man is expected to comply with whatever a woman desire is to make her interested based on the moment in order to commence with sexual callings. Most new men are expected to have personal all-around success with his family. Some new men are even asked to answer to their significant other as the head of house. Does the new man even know who he is, or what he is doing as he is evolving? We'll ask him later (See my upcoming book "For Men Only.")

Now women have much more expectations from relationships. Women want relationships to be purposeful, meaningful, passionate, adventures, spiritual, mysterious, erotic and always advancing. Now women set the rules and expectations for most relationships. Many women want men to be a partner, friend, confidant, provider, co-parents, romantic interest, caregivers, passionate lover and a very responsible person. Men want women to have a good attitude, get along and be feminine.

Relationships are now a romantic enterprise for pleasure and connection and no longer for family and dependency.

CHAPTER 7
THE MILLENNIAL MAN

Some millennial's and others may believe that one of the ways to value yourself as a millennial man is to embrace and express your feelings. The old-school or traditional masculine man was taught and shown not to embrace and express his feeling. It seems the millennial man has been convinced this is a way to connect and really get to know yourself. Many millennial men may believe that if one doesn't embrace and express himself, they are hiding or denying their feelings. Some millennial men may believe in order to become who you are supposed to be is to connect with your emotional curiosity. By doing this you will discover your uniqueness. I believe your uniqueness is derived from your personality and your interpretation of your perception of life.

It may appear the millennial man has walked away from the traditional male role of provider, protector and cultivator. More importantly the masculinity disposition of a man. The millennial man has conformed to the new now concepts. These new concepts are loosely defined as many things such as, stay at home father, we are partners, your outer-self is aligned with your inner-self, be vulnerable, express your feeling, I need to be heard and it's not about being manly but equal. The millennial man who many believes it's ok for a woman to purse him or vis-verse. Many millennial men believe it is ok for the woman to support and take care of him. Some millennial men believe their feeling are just as important as his woman's, and she should always consider his feeling in the relationship as much as her feelings. What!!

Most millennial men believe they shouldn't just strive economically, and everything should be equal and fair 50/50 in the relationship. They also, believe they should be valued as much as the women in the relationship with attention, time and gifts. Some believe it is ok to be it all, whatever a woman can do I can do. The home maker and braid his daughter's hair, the main provider and remain sensitive and cry with pride.

Today's views and expectations of masculinity and the definition of what is manly is slowly dissipating. The average millennial man aggressively accepts and considers caregiving to children and to the household should be an equal responsibility with the spouses. Or more so better handled as the man's responsibility. Many millennial men agree that the woman should carry more of the financial responsibility in the relationship.

I believe that the millennial man has lost or chosen not to become ambitious and take the lead position while in a relationship. With little ambitious the millennial man embraces staying at home playing video games while his girl goes out and works all day. I believe the millennial man has lost or given up on having self-respect and the respect of others on how he carries himself. Not considering any set of principles or certain rules a man should live by. With no or low self-respect, it doesn't matter how he dresses, if he earns income, if he is able to take care of his responsibilities or respected by others. It's about, if he feels good about himself, that makes it ok. Some millennial men think it is ok if he is not masculine or stands up for his girl in danger, she can call 911 right. It's sad to believe that some millennial men have no moral reservation with having multiple children by multiple women and be a dad to none of them. It seems the accountability of the millennial man has very little concern for himself or the future.

The complete millennial generation men and women display a lazy, entitled, and self-centered behavior and way of life. This generation of people is growing up with so much advance technology, having an abundance of everything, a high self-esteem of I deserve, I deserve. Both men and women put much of their interest in social connections with friends and having resources to things as most important. And not self-development, principles and the respect of others. The millennial generation leaves little to having respect and responsibility to themselves. These types of actions and concepts have also mostly affected the women in this generation. Because of the "new now" concepts of the millennial generation of entitlement and self-centered behavior this have caused an increase in the single parent homes today. Because the family structure has changed since the 1960's women prospective on two household parenting is perceived to not be a big deal.

CHAPTER 8
THE SINGLE PARENT HOUSEHOLD

Approximately ten to twenty percent of the homes in America are ran by single mothers and approximate fifteen percent of other homes are integrated without their biological father.

Many may disagree that women are the direct cause of the single parent home. I believe this is primarily because to bring life in this world the woman has the first and last say so. As a woman being the main contributor of the breakdown of the two-parent household structure; it makes it difficult the man to see the value in the woman in order for her getting what she wants from a man. I strongly believe that every family need both a mother and father spite what many women may believe. Women don't need men and how they can be the man and woman of their family. This doesn't work.

Many years ago, single parent households were contributed mainly to poor women and minorities. Today single parenthood is becoming a part of the new "norm." Regardless of economic condition or situations that would apply to why someone who is a single parent. Many of the millennial's and others has a different outlook on poverty and single parenthood today. Many of the millennial's view poverty as someone who can't get what they need to survive. Rather than being in a financial condition that lacks the essential resources of a minimum standard of living. Basically, not having enough money to meet your basic needs for life's daily necessities for the day. Many of the millennial consider single parenthood as just a choice or another way to parent.

Many single mothers today may feel empowered to be a single mom. The satisfaction of governing all the choices and concerns of your child without any challenges can be commanding. One main reason many women gravitate to the new "norm" of single parenthood is building a tight-knit relationship with their children and not sharing them with others. Having that complete control. Also, knowing you are the sole parent to having all your hard work payoff to a successful child is very rewarding. Never needing to negotiate, or just being the sole role model can be fulfilling. Maybe the most satisfying for many women is bestowing your own value, belief and concepts without compromise. Whatever the reason the research shows how much a child lacks socially, emotionally and many times financially without the other parent. Because of the many forms of contraception for women that this choice has been taken too lightly. I believe women has the ultimate control over introducing a baby life to the world with regarding her fertility.

We hear and see it through the media often throughout the years, most woman if given a choice would be in a committed relationship or marriage. If this is the case, why for the past forty to sixty years single women has been the majority in parenting our children in this country. Many of these single women have been telling and showing their daughters to become independent and strong. Go out and get your higher education and become a good wage earner. And many of these single women have been showing their son's how they go through man after man after man, and how easy it will be for them as a man to bounce from woman to woman without the repercussions and right-now responsibilities of life. It seems that the modern woman has focus their actions and desire away from being a good mate for a man, and society has conditioned these women to believe they can do and have anything they want. This haven't been proven true. Be independent, be independent, be independent.

These women are training their daughters to believe that their value is in their education and income. It's not! Men don't care about your money or your education. Men care if you are kind to them, that you speak to them with respect and carry yourself as a respect lady. Men care if they can get along with you and you are able to hold your peace. These women are showing their sons and daughters men don't have to be provider and leaders of their household. Many women are showing their daughters it's more important to speak your mind and express the value of your thoughts than to get along. You must be heard! The media also is telling these women they deserve a man that will provide for her and her children, a man who is honorable, ethical, be faithful, be an ongoing giver showering her with gifts, be compassionate, a man who respects her and her opinions, a man of integrity and intelligence who has a purpose in life. But you still can't get along with a man. The media is telling these women not to settle for the average, you deserve the best. Girl don't settle for average! When in fact most of our population is average. Therefore, these are some of the reasons many of the households are ran by single women and many women will remain man less. Women are continually telling their daughters not to settle and showing them how not to get along with a man. Focus on your education!!

Women want all these things but chooses not to be kind to her man when things aren't going the way she like. Sadly, we don't hear the media telling women they should be submissive, helpful to her man and guard her togue with the negative repercussion of her words. Or simply just try to get along with your man. Sadly, we don't hear the media telling women that at twenty years old you shouldn't expect to be in the same position with a couple of their fifties. Sadly, we don't hear the media telling women they can't remain the same independent mindset when they were alone, then in a marriage. Women are told and shown many ways how they don't have to get along and that everything should go their way. What kind of partnership is that?

Happy Wife, Happy Life!! Have this work?

CHAPTER 9
WHAT IS THE PARTNERSHIP IN A RELATIONSHIP?

Yes, in a since he or she is your partner. But not the way the mainstream media and social media portrays how a partner supposed to be. In the past fifty years or so the media has developed this new concept in relationships that couples are partners. If we consider the nature of a natural relationship there is a union of two to be of one idea, one vision, and one image that of a couple. Not a collaboration of two to be partners link together for each one's benefit. A true partnership in a relationship both share equal liabilities, responsibilities and equal benefits in the relationship. Where two people share in equal endeavors and equal or similar risk in the relationship. Also, as partners the position of accountability, obligation and outcome are presumed to be equal or similar in value. To consider this one may believe that each person shares equal needs and desires. If not, can this truly be a partnership?

In a natural relationship the needs and desires of a man and woman are different. Man and woman value and express different things in a relationship. Here are some examples, women normally are more intuitive, flexible, and sociable then men. Who need personal devotion, affection, to be cherished, and much attention? Men are normally more consistent, simple and rational then women. Who need respect, appreciation, sex and to display his masculine disposition? Men need to achieve and accomplish things and prove his competence. Women need to feel appreciated and fulfilled through her relationships. So far it doesn't seem equal. Men need to be problem solvers rather than seek help for his problems. Women need to express themselves and be heard and seek help for her problems. Men feel sometimes threatened by expression of their feelings. Women need attention and constant expression of her feeling. Men need respect and less drama, chaos and conversation. So far different needs and outcomes. Men usually don't want his woman to change when the get together and women usually want to change her man. Men appreciate and desires a woman to need him in many ways. Woman appreciate and desire a man to want, love and cherish her. Women want sympathy, and men usually offer resolutions. Men need women not to pressure him with accomplishments and change. Women appreciate and desire a man who they can depend on in every way in the relationship. Basically, support or supply all her emotional needs. Men mostly don't want his emotional needs met or discussed. Men need a woman to know how important to never disrespect him with her words. Women need men who they can depend on for support and validation. These needs and desires don't seem to be equal in any way.

Women really want a man to stand by his word when says he is going to do this or that. A woman wants to believe a man will always conduct himself in a manner that will always show respect to her, no matter what. Women want to feel you are proud that you landed her and always represent her proudly when you introduce her. Women want to feel number one in a man's life over everyone else. Period.

Men need women to respect his decision even when it may or may not be the best decision. A woman needs a man who she can come to when things are going wrong and she can express herself to where he can validate the way she is feeling. Women need a man who can take or share responsibilities without having her feeling overwhelm. Men needs a woman to always show herself with self-respect to him when she is in public. Women needs a man who can commit and act in dedicating time and attention to her. Men need women to believe in him and not what his plans or situation is. A man needs his woman to need him to facilitate the relationship because of his authority as a man. Women needs a man to want to give to her because she is valuable to him.

As we discussed some of the differences of a men and women, it may be difficult to believe relationships as an equal partnership. A partner or partnership is express as they should be equal in some way. In a natural relationship they should never be considered equal only unique in their nature as a man or woman. Combining their difference and needs to one union under one leader for one pledge with one vision. Because men and women are unmatched in their thinking and unlike in their emotions and driven differently by their will, they are only partners as being together not as functioning equals.

The new concepts of today's relationships manipulate men and women believing in partnership that is equal, yet many women still want everything to go their way. Again, living the mindset, Happy Wife, Happy Life! I ask, why women act this way?

CHAPTER 10
WHY WOMEN ACT THIS WAY

For most years' most societies have allowed the very beautiful women of the world to have anything they wanted. This widespread behavior only exists because of the nature of a man, and his desires that is driven by his eyes in regard to women. Since the beginning of time the powerful and the elite has primarily been men. Because of this they have afforded the beautiful women of the world to live in this unrealistic bubble of reality. To say, do, and get almost anything they want. Not that this is right in any way it's just these men played their power to their favor. Because of being a privilege woman, these types of women didn't experience any serious consequences with bad behavior or demanding their personal desires. If they wanted something, they just got it. If they did something that wasn't appropriate it was accepted or overlooked. They never received that slap on the wrist or disciplined for doing wrong. In their world there was no wrong only what I deserve, and I deserve it for being me.

For the past twenty plus years or so in America our new social society has circulated this mindset thru the media that every woman deserves what she wants. Yes, I deserve it. And every woman deserves the best. Yes, I deserve it. It has been presumed no longer you needed to be privilege from wealth, beautiful, elite, or extremely attractive woman to get what you deserve. This has been basically a learned behavior in this and many countries. No longer the wealthy and elite can experience this type of idealistic lifestyle and mindset. Not anymore.

For many women today it seems they have developed the learned mindset and behavior, I deserve it. Many women believe they deserve the best of the best, easy going life, and so on. They think they deserve it merely by existing, just because they are a woman. It appears that women love telling other women they deserve it as well. Most people can see and hear it everywhere. What I hear the most is girl you deserve to be treated like a queen. Do most girls act like queens that you know? I'm sure most people have heard girl you deserve a better car, a better man, a better job, a better ring, just because they are women. I've yet to hear a man says to another man you deserve whatever, just because you are a man. Almost every man may believe they need to earn whatever they get. Unless it's a gift.

What about the clear and obvious behavior of women daily? Should they ignore the way they are and simple acknowledge, I am a woman? Women you deserve chocolate when you are cranky, mad, and disrespectful. Women you deserve a five-thousand-dollar ring when you consistently mismanage money, don't get along with your mate, and you can't afford it. Women you deserve a better man when you don't listen to him, don't value his wisdom, and disrespects him in public. Women you deserve to be treated like a queen when you dress promiscuous, you throw temper tantrums, and express yourself with no regard to other people's feelings. My point is this modern-day woman has adapted a mindset regardless of her morals and behavior that she deserves it!

Women please don't be offended be enlighten. Hopefully the women in who this is directed to can slowly and carefully examine themselves to develop a better you, to make a better us. I know men are not perfect nor am I saying they are better in any way. I believe this may be the biggest problem in which women are not getting what they want from a man. I just want to hold up the mirror for those of you to see if you have adapted this mindset to hopefully change for a better life. Let it go! I think every woman should be treated with excellent, but not just because you are a woman. None of us deserve what's not warranted to us.

This is another, why women act this way that is preventing them from getting what they want from a man. Many times, women enter a relationship they try or do take over the man's responsibility. Many women believe that if he is not doing it, I'll do it. Why? Because it needs to be done and she must do it. And so, she does. This does not put you or the man in a better place in the relationship and this takes you both out of your element.

Women stop demanding and commanding things from and to your man. This does not work. Right? You have been doing it for so long and you are tired. Because it hasn't changed. Why? You need to realize if he wasn't doing it from the beginning, he's probably not going to start doing it because you said so. You must be reasonable when it comes down to people's behavior because it derives from habits and habits from our mindset. Only the person with the mindset can change their mindset. So, why women act this way? They believe the man will change.

Women do not go into a relationship to repair someone or needing repair yourself. We are all flawed to some degree, but no one should enter a relationship not whole, not fully single, and unaware of their strength and weakness. Be accountable for your short comings and ability of doing your work on you. Women don't disregard your insecurities while focusing on your man's insecurities when entering or in a relationship. Don't be dismissive to your man's basic needs.

Many women approach a man or relationship with the mindset I have my own. I have my own this and that I don't need you.

A woman's value is not in her education or economics. A man sees her value is in her touch, the way she speaks to him and her physical physic showing separate from his. The way she is kind, delate and tactful to him and others. For these reasons, a man seeks after a woman.

Since the times have change women are more convince, they no longer need a man. Many years ago, women needed men to provide and protect them. Because we live in an era of economic opportunity and individual independence many women may see men as obsolete. Great jobs, higher education, and a multitude of opportunities are at the fingertips of most women today. Traveling has become so easy and affordable to do alone. Women today can even get a sperm donor or have a one-night stand to procreate if necessary, to have children. So, it really seems like women just don't need a man! Independent, modern, and successful women appear to everywhere; with the media help it looks very difficult for any women to be convinced they need a man. The main ideology promoted among women today gives the impression your primary goal in life is a successful career. Maybe this is the main cause women act the way they act.

Yet we see it time and time again, women rushing down the isle to get married. Do women really know what they want?

CHAPTER 11
DO WOMEN KNOW WHAT THEY WANT?

I have been asking this question over twenty years. Because of my personal pursuit this question has been on the forefront of many conversations. I would speak to teenagers all the way up to the elders (80's). Most women claim they know what they want. Many women petition they just need someone who is willing to meet them where they are (financially). Someone to treat them as equals and share their time and interest with them. A man that can be a true partner with a rational sensitivity and understanding of how to treat them. Many women say they need a man to provide them with financial, emotional and practical support. Woman say they need a man who is sensitive, emotional supportive, understanding, and someone who respects them. They say they don't need a masculine and macho man just someone who communicate regularly and tactfully. They say they want a friendship with their man. Someone who is emotionally mature even if they're not, and sensitivity is essential. Also, someone who can bring adventure and excitement into the relationship and someone who is open to new experiences. Some women want men to be feminist allies in their lives with equality for their success.

Many women say they want a man who makes her feel safe and secure, but not to masculine. To feel safe and secure with little actions like, paying attention when she is cold, irritable, or uncomfortable. To feel safe and secure when you're out in public by holding her hand and asking how she is feeling. To feel safe and secure when you check on her to make sure she made it home safe when she's not with you. Probably, the main way to make her feel safe and secure is to stand up for her and make sure she is treated well when she is dealing with anyone.

Women say if she finds a man who will treat her as equals and share their time and interest with her. Treat her with mutual respect sensitivity and understanding and a man keeping the romantic spark burning. A man who provide her with emotional support with everyday life's issues and willing to meet her where she is.

Yes, it sounds like a woman want a lot! And yes, this may be all true but if you gave a woman some of these things and no financial security, it's not enough. Or if you give a woman half these things, it's not enough. What a woman really want is what she really needs financial and emotional security. Basically, the primary need of women is financial security even if she needs to get it herself. So, everything else without that doesn't matter as much. Most woman will choose security and stability over all else because of a woman's nature of self-preservation. That's why most women want that "High Value Man."

TODAY'S HIGH VALUE MAN

I believe as I got older and more aware, I realized the behavior of a person and the conditioning of a person's needs will always supersede what a person wants. I began to pay closer attention to what women really needed to properly function and to excel. Because of the natural fear of ending up alone and the desire for the comfort in life most women would seek the things that would offer security above all else. What women really want is having financial security as the number one need, if nothing else. So, many women would focus on these things just in case they never get that high value man like, their education and work ethics or anything that would bring financial security, while still thinking they are pursuing a high value man.

Most women really want a high value man. A high value man today is considered a man of power, influence and financial security. A man who believes he can do, be or have anything he puts his mind to. A man the thinks and behaves independently financially, emotionally and mentally, with options and financial favor.

One of the misconceptions that many women have in their twenties and thirties with trying to find high value man is finding a man in their same age group. Unless a woman finds an entertainer or an athlete of that sorts at that age she is, not practical. Most men don't start maturing until they get in their late forties and early fifties. What this means is about ninety-nine out of every one hundred men you meet in their twenties until their late thirties will not be a "High Value Man."

Another misconception woman have is if they could find a "High Value Man" in their age group they wouldn't have the respect for that man that is needed to solidify the relationship. A high valued man will expect you to treat and think of him and his needs first with care and concern, regardless how you feel. Always respect and listen to him and give him the courtesy of what he says, with respect. A high vale man will expect his woman to respect and know his physical and emotional boundaries and stay in her lane. To respect him by how she carrier herself by how she dresses, act and look according to his desires. Considering these actions for a woman of twenty- or thirty-years old dealing with a man of the same age would be almost impossible to respect him like this.

Another misconception as a woman is not making many changes to fit the needs of a high value man. Many women may think that she can find a high value man and he is to accept her as she is. I don't think so. A high value man will have expectations. Like, giving up many if not all your friends and social life that's does not condition or aligns with his lifestyles. Also, if you are not conditioned to maintain your weight and looks as a priority for a high value man, you would need to adjust. Sometimes a woman may need to relocate if you are not in the same area of her man.

One of the most challenging things a woman may need to face when trying to acquire a high vale man is giving up her authority over her children she is bringing to the relationship.

Many may argue women prefer to be single. Although, I haven't seen or heard any evidence to support that idea. I believe most women prefer to be in a relationship and not be single. If this is the case one would believe that women would have more control over their fertility. A woman's fertility gives or removes many of her options with gaining a high value man. But because of the government's influence and the media's manipulation have many women today believing they are more impowered by having children, even out of wedlock. Yet, many women have created what they believe would help them to weed out the looser from the high vale men. "The Checklist."

CHAPTER 12
THE CHECKLIST

I'm not sure where or when this started but most women have a checklist when looking for a man. Especially, the high value man. I believe a lot of women have a checklist for every man she is potentially interested in. I believe there are different checklists that most of these women have. There may be a checklist is to track how often a man does things for her. There may be a checklist is a list of requirements that a woman wants everything to fit in with her or the way she feels. There may be a checklist of real substance like values and behavior traits.

I believe that most women have the right intentions when making a checklist. Maybe they don't want to get out of control with the way they feel for a guy. Especially when the guy seems too good to be true. Maybe it's a way for them not to forget what's important. Maybe it's just a reality check. Here is some example of a woman's typical checklist:

Does he complement me?   Is he attractive to me?
Is he supportive?   Can I have a real conversation with him?
Is he dependable?   Is he transparent?
Is he ambitious?   Does he want family?
Do we have the same beliefs?   Do our futures align?
Is he considerate?   Is he romantic?
Is he adventurous?   Does he enjoy all foods?
Does he want to spend quality time with me?

What type of job does he have?   Is he a good listener?

Do we have chemistry?   Is he stable?

Is he cheap?   Is he in touch with his emotions?

These are the most importance questions or qualities I have heard women tell me for a checklist. Although, their intentions may be right some women base this checklist with personality traits to find out if the guy is right for them. Most of these on the list are valid but, more important it is not to discover if you and your guy are compatible. It all comes down to finding if you both fit. Now let's take a look below at the other type of checklists.

Even with the requirement checklist I believe there are two different ones based on two different types of women. One type of woman looking for things of the surface and superficial that reveals unrealistic and self-centered desires. The other type of checklist is trying to find someone with the best fit. The first type of woman's checklist has good intensions. This next may be full of surface desires and superficial things. Like, what type of car does he drive? Or he must drive a certain type of car. Does he have swagger and dress with the current trends? Or he must ware certain name-brands clothing. Does he have a high-powered job? Or he must have this type or that type of job. Does he have influence and financial security? Or he must own his own home located in a certain area. Does he live a luxury lifestyle? Or he needs to be able to take me to the fine restaurants and be able to travel abroad. Does he have children, and how many? Or he can't have children or no more than one. These are some of the many questions on the checklist from many women looking for a checklist man.

The problem with this type of checklist is it represent no substance for the man she is only interested in what she wants for herself, not the relationship. Most women with this type of checklist doesn't even have what it takes to get or keep this type of man. Many times, women don't consider when they are looking for all these materialist and superficial things in a man, they are two. These types of men expect on demand your time and corporation because they know you are high maintenance. And they are paying for it. Because they bring so much to the table they expect you to treat them with the utmost respect. Also, many of them require you to cater to them from head to foot. These types of guys require you to be fit and in shape with a good attitude all the time. Your appearance represents them at all times. These types of men think because I provide and take care of everything his needs come first, regardless how you feel. These types of men expect you to know his physical and emotional boundaries and stay in your lane. So, ladies be careful when you have such a materialist demanding checklist because it always comes with a cost.

The other checklist of requirements is for those women who keeps notes and track of how often he does things for her. She may track how often he takes her to diner and the quality of restaurant. She may track or require him to bring her flowers weekly. I believe the worst is if she is making a change list. This is things she needs him to change in order them to continue to go forward. This may consist of her dislikes about his looks, car he drives, down to his demeanor. Or a list that require him to meet that fulfills her desire. This type of list shows a woman controlling and many possible insecurities.

There was a TV show I believe it aired on December 8, 2016 on the "Steve Harvey Show." Steve Harvey meets and interviews a woman named Heather. Heather, "who says she can't find a man who meets her requirements." Heather has been dating for the past eight years looking for someone to meet these requirements. Heather presents this short (Lol) list below to Steve. "Steve, says to Heather he doesn't know if this person exists." Heather, responded "No, he got to exist, you don't think so." Steve replied, "let me ask you something, it has been eight years do you have another eight years to do like the last eight." I believe Heather is one of many women believing they can and deserve to get everything they want, without surrendering to her nature state. Or providing good benefits to her man in order to receive what she wants. Meaning if she wanted to receive all these ridiculous things what is she willing to do? Here's Heather's list:

Must be age 30 to 45

Must be financially stable

No children

Height between 5' 10" or taller

No hook ups or flings

Must be ready to settle down

No roommates

Non-smoker

Must love desserts

Can't be anti-sugar

Must be honest

Must be reliable

Must be sweet and kind

Must be quick-witted

Must be romantic

Must love food

Must pay on the first date

No flowers on the first date

Must be a social drinker

Must never wear sweatpants

Must be adventures

Must be spontaneous

Must be a planner

Can't be self-centered

Can't be cocky Not intimidated by me

Must love dogs Favorite season not fall

Can't own a dog from a breeder

Can't be jealous of her dog

Can't own a cat

Must be in shape

Can't have six-pack abs

Can't be too skinny

Can't have a runner's physique

Can't be stronger than me

Can't be a hunter

Can't be obsessed with sports

Can't be a hunter

Can't own a boat

Can't be a gamer

Can't be materialistic

Must respect a gluten-free diet

Can't be too close to family and friends

Must open doors for me

Must be willing to move someplace warm

Must love traveling

Can't brag about traveling

Must maintain eye contact

Can't be a party boy

Wow! And this isn't the complete list. Sometimes some women can get so carried away with this "checklist" they forget how self-centered it can become. Although Heather mentioned she wanted a man that wasn't self-centered. Image that. Even as ridiculous as this list may appear, I believe Heather could get what she wants. But I don't believe Heater present herself as the person that is willing to do what she needs to get what she wants. She quickly mentioned in the interview with Steve that she has her Own Business, and, in a way, she's basically set in her ways. When she said it, to me, she implied a since of entitlement. Like if a High-valued man would say to a woman not at his economic level, "this is what my requirements are." Meet them or I'll find someone who will.

I believe it's good for a woman to have a checklist. Be careful when making your list it shouldn't be too long. Make sure your checklist is things of principle and healthy behavior traits. For example, I listed below my suggested Top 10 checklist for a woman:

Is he honest and transparent?
How does he communicate, and is he a good listener?
Does he live a trustworthy life?
Does his friends and family respect him?
Does he forgive easy?
Does he make me comfortable being me?
Does he believe the same philosophy as me with intimacy?
How does he manage money?
Is he on the same page with me regarding children?
Do we have an understanding with both our e-life?

CHAPTER 13
DATING

Dating, I'm going to try to be short with this chapter. I'm just going to try an touch on a few points, because dating is a book in it-self. Many may tell you about dating, is to date multiple people, have a checklist, have short dates, have a set of dating rules of do's and don'ts, and most important be upfront about what you want.

Most people or even some experts will tell you that dating today is complicated. I disagree. I say that because I believe the success of dating all lye's before you start dating. It can be complicate only if you are not prepared to engage in the dating arena.

I believe dating begins with self. Meaning you need to honest with yourself about what you want, need and intend to do while dating. Once you have done that you need to setup a set of questions that you intend to ask each person that you will potentially date. These types of questions need to reveal if you and the other person will be a good fit. Your trying to find out if their life will align with your life without either one of you making any significant changes. You also want to ask a set of questions that will demonstrate how well the person deals with life's challenges and conflict. You should determine if you both are looking for short-term or long-term expectations while dating. Maybe the most important questions to ask is about their core values and daily behaviors. Not common interest like, do you like the movies, or if the are sports fans, and other commonalities. These types of questions won't help either of you.

Let's say they are sports fans or even extreme sports fans and you are not. You should find out how committed to be a fan is, do they replace sports as one of the core values. If so, that should be a warning sign. Let's say he is an extreme extended family man. Meaning he is always spending time and helping his extended family and that's something you are not interested in. Maybe you are the type of person that believes in putting immediate family first all the time. Let's say you guys have been talking over the phone for weeks and you discover he is not a forgiving person based on his past experiences. And you can't be with a type of person like that. Maybe during your phone conversations, he expresses how bad he is with money, no one should start dating or a relationship with someone who isn't good with managing their money. Find out if you guys are on the same page with how you spend your time with your e-life. Whatever it is all this should be done before you guys go on your first date. The more you know about each other before you start dating in person the better the outcome.

Most people approach dating with many boundaries and insecurities already there. Most of us focus on not getting hurt or looking stupid, we forget to focus on the important things. Know yourself before you start dating and know what question and answers you are looking for. People focus more on right now then doing what is right. For these reasons, many of us end up alone.

CHAPTER 14
THE FEAR OF ENDING UP ALONE

This may be one of the biggest fears we all face. Rather it's a fear of being unwanted and alone or if it is a fear of being without the one, we love and lonely. Because of this many people create unhealthy habits behind this type of mindset. Some people who think this may convince themselves to do whatever it takes not to be alone. Maybe they may believe their happiness and completeness comes from someone else, and it doesn't. A lot of times people find themselves quickly getting into relationships without really knowing the other person. Others may convince themselves to stay in unhealthy relationships, so they won't be lonely. The media is constantly feeding people the need to have a someone in their life and sadly this mindset starts within our children, and sometimes before their teens.

If you feel fearful of being alone, you need to address it immediately. When someone has a fear of be alone that fear can cause anger, anxiety, and sometimes impact their daily thinking in negative ways. Most of the time fear of being alone comes from lack of controlling your emotions or not being comfortable with who you are. You need to practice on changing your mindset. Exercise things like, acknowledging some of the benefits of not having someone to be accountable to. Another way is appreciating the time you have by including hobbies and finding new interest. The key is finding the balance in your mind, so you can change how you see the time you spend with yourself. Also, don't continue to engage in the same behavior that previously made you feel alone or unwanted. Like, if being on Facebook all day make you feel alone, stop. One of the best things to do is consistently engage in things that helps you meet people and helping other people in need.

Being alone and single does not mean you need to be lonely. Being lonely only means you have not developed the skills to become whole. Whole meaning you do not need anyone to complete you or make you feel good about spending time with yourself. The thin line between being alone and lonely is a state of mind. Because many couples are with someone and still feel lonely.

Being alone is a time to appreciate your time and learn how to best manage your time. Being alone is a time to enjoy the time you have and use it to grow who you are. This is a time to set priorities in your life to reduce stress and gain focus. Also setting priorities can improve your productivity and help manage what you want. With no alone time you will not be able to balance a healthy life. I think the most important thing about being alone is helping yourself to identify what you truly need and appreciate in your life. When a person doesn't have enough time alone it can be difficult to understand and manage your finances. Meaning if you have months or years of being single you may have more practice on being accountable to managing your money than someone who has been in a relationship right out of high school. Many people don't know money management is a learned behavior. The longer you are single you can develop skill sets on how to manage friendships. The longer you are single you will become better dealing with all sorts of relationships. Also, being single helps you respect and appreciate not just yours's but other people space. These are some ways to become whole.

Another way to fight fear of being alone is respecting your time by preparing, practicing, and improving who you are. So, you can see yourself not alone, just not tiedown. Good people who are searching for someone is always looking for someone of value. This is the time to become valuable. By increasing your experiences and life's lessons makes you much more valuable than one who has none. Practice managing your responses to your emotions. One should focus on learning multiple work trades, travel as much as they can, create hobbies and engage in multiple interesting adventures. Expand your knowledge on history, science and different cultures. Maybe learn a different language. Maybe get involved in local social events. Take up hiking or some sporting activity. Plan to take an inexpensive weekend cruise. Get in a hot air balloon ride or a helicopter tour. I believe one of the most enriching things to do is to increase your prospective of understanding men. Also, giving your time to others increases your value and to volunteer your time to any worthy cause gives a better sense of you to you. Basically, the more interesting you are and the most experienced you are at dealing with life's opportunity, challenges and situations the more valuable you will become as a person. People like people who can add, increase or bring interest and excitement to their lives. Most of these types of people are healthy single people, by choice.

Being alone is not a problem that needs to be fixed. Being alone is something to understand how to deal with as a natural part of life. Our culture has taught us one of the most important things is not to be alone when experiencing pain, suffering and loss. Which is true, we shouldn't be alone when dealing with these conditions. Many of us look to others that have been through what we are experiencing to cope with. This type of fear drives many people no matter what, is not to be alone to experience the loneliness. Many people may confuse being alone with loneliness. God made us to be co-depended, so we don't feel the loneliness. So, we naturally look to others for this need, when in fact God wanted us to look to him, to be co-depended on Him.

CHAPTER 15
THE SUBTLE DIFFERENCES BETWEEN MEN & WOMEN

Hello women, before we get started with the "How to get what you want from man," chapter, allow me talk about some of the characteristic and basic behaviors of a man for those who may not know. Let's me give you what I have learned, and I will explain how men process information differently from a woman. Let's establish some of the oppositions of men and women facing the same situation, and how they see it differently and respond differently. Also, we will talk about men having fewer connections between their left and right brain hemispheres, and what that means. These examples are not to claim how different men and women think and emote rather to reveal an understanding on how we can better relate.

These are some of the basic characteristic of a man. Men don't like being defeated. Men don't like being challenged by their significant other. Men like and need to provide and have someone depend on them. Men need to pursue a woman to embrace their authoritative disposition. A man's nature and behavior are to deny most emotions in order to be able to make rational decisions. Men take pleasure in intellectual issues and challenges. A man naturally is competitive and prideful.

Here is some example of men basic behaviors when dealing with hostility, disagreement, disapproval, and challenges. Men usually deal with hostility differently with stranger than friends and love ones. For example, if men are dealing with their wives or partners, they tin to get more emotional and often use anger as their go-to for expression and actions. Men usually have more patience and restraint when dealing with strangers. When men are dealing with disagreements and normal challenges, they tin to remain rational and unemotional while trying to withdraw from the situation before it elevates. Constant disapproval to a man is like, you no longer like him and normally a man will distant himself from that person.

How men and women process things differently. When a woman is faced with difficulty or a problem, her brain connects with her emotions to show and express empathy. She will then try to understand or reach out for understanding and sympathy. She will want to know why and receive compassion from others. More importantly her brain will tell her why he doesn't feel this way. She will want you to feel how she feels. – When a man is going thru difficulties or having a problem, he too will experience empathy, but the male brain does not respond when he or someone is expressing problems rather his brain goes to the "fix-it" section. Men are more concern with fixing a problem than showing harmony in feelings. Men and women's brains process, computes, and respond to emotional events differently. When women experience emotional events, they usually remember minute details of the complete situation while men usually cannot recall most if not any of the details. This is because men usually shut down the emotional memory related areas that connect to the right and left part of the brain.

Here is an example about the oppositions of men and women facing the same situation, and how they see it differently and respond differently. I'm using the first example from my first book. If you guys decide to go out on the town tonight and you both get dressed and leave from home together all is well. when you guys get home and walk thru the door and what she sees is not what he sees. Meaning she may see that the house is out if order and the things they may be out of place and so on. What he might see is nothing wrong, and he didn't notice anything out of order and so on.

CHAPTER 16
THE SHORT STORY

As the many years has past many men has been silently screaming out for women to need them again. Most women realize they don't need a man, yet they consistently demonstrate they want a man and for this reason women don't use your gifts as a weapon against a man. Most women are told even before their teenage years to enjoy their singlehood focus on their career, spend money, travel and enjoy hanging out with their friends. Some women are even told not to focus on a man just their 5-year or 10-year plan. This may be how some people and most of society have told women how to behave and see themselves, but the real reality is we exist here for each other. As men and women, we have an innate fundamental desire for connecting with one another by design.

Women be proud of being a woman soft, tactful, and delicate it makes you more attractive. That is who you are deep down inside by nature. Women you should want to embrace your feminine energy created from the inside because that is your power. Your femininity is not based on your clothing, make-up, shoes, education, or money. For the women who choose to find your way back to your true femininity it's self-love and acceptance thru your expression. Your femininity derives from your energy and how you express it. To express yourself, you create your environment around you with your elegance, charm, and grace. Always embrace your emotions because you are designed to. Your feminine disposition is moved by your emotions and the way you are loved. Don't be confused on how you should act be feminine always tactful and easy to get along with. In order to remain feminine in challenging situations you must live by a set of rules that tells you to act pleasant and easy to work with before the challenging situation every exist. Being feminine isn't being passive rather about receiving and being certain of how you express your demeanor. One big factor many women have abandon is the ability to lean back and let go. This is a powerful and unique gift that was given to the femininity for women. Use it.

Many years ago, women didn't have to concern themselves about the economic and domestic challenges of the world. Because of the many changes in society women have adapted the constant stressing and worrying of the daily dealing of life. Which has caused them to forget how to lean back. Women stop trying to act like you are worthy just show yourself to feminine. Many times, women who seek higher education and enter the workforce while taking on many responsibilities and add many stressors it affects your feminine energy. You must learn to separate your attachment or take on less responsibilities. Nothing should be more important to you than losing your femininity except your spirituality. Nothing. It's like taking an apple tree and try to make it produce oranges, it's not natural. If that tree doesn't know how to produce oranges, it won't be well. If a woman is not standing in her complete element of womanhood eventually, she malfunctions. Basically, emotions are the essence of femininity, and to feel something you need to surrender to something. Being feminine is part of being a woman. It's OK. Use it.

OK, we are ready for you to get what you want from a man.

CHAPTER 17
THE SUMMARY

HOW TO GET WHAT YOU WANT FROM A MAN

I believe any man you are dealing with you can get what you want from him if it is within him means. Rather it is someone you been with a short time or been with for years. Now, if you have been with someone for years and you or him, has animosity, resentment, or share many hurtful experiences this may not be the time to experience this. If people in relationship do not heal from this type of pain your relationship will not be healthy. I suggest that you or both see a therapist to resolve your issues. For all others let's continue.

I know you though it wasn't true, but it is. There are four phases I recognized thru my soulmate experience if practice as a part of your foundation in your relationship with your man you will get what you want. The four phases are learning and speaking a man's language, giving him quality time for him, provide acts of service only for him and sex, self and surprise. If you incorporate these technics as part of your foundation in your relationship it will produce a healthy outcome for the both of you, while you get what you want.

PHASE 1

First is to learn to speak his language. Many women may think I'm about to tell you to learn how to speak his love language, No. Women have a love language, not men. I know you have been told wrong! Seriously I'm giving you exactly what you need to get exactly what you want. Stay with me. The language men appreciate and recognize is short, direct, with kindness and much respect. Just express it with your femininity, you know. Also, speaking a man language is to give him verbal appreciation and approval. For an example, when you show your appreciation it should be from a place that you are pleased with him. Always thanking him and being thankful of him. Show him how relieved you are in his life, stay in the moment. Also, when showing your approval of him is never trying to change him or the way he is doing it. Even when it's not the way you want, you just except him. If you always speak his type of language with him...you are on the way in getting what you want. Now, he's thinking I can't believe how easily she is satisfied with me. Phase one complete.

PHASE 2

Next you need to commit to quality time. This may not be the most important thing to him, but you need to do it and make him feel it's the most important thing to you. Meaning the more you express thru your femininity to him that your time together once a week or so with him is priceless the more he will feel loved by you. Why? Because he now thinks you need him. For instance, don't just sit at home for TV time like regular, make an activity or place that will allow you to focus your attention only on him. Phase two complete.

PHASE 3

If you are a busy person still, try to manage a set time or day of each week and provide an act of service. This means, something that you do for him each week that he can look forward to. For example, it could be as simple as cooking his favorite meal, picking up his laundry, cutting his hair, giving him a massage or whatever, it is he enjoys or can reduce his stress from the week. Be consistent. Phase three complete.

PHASE 4

This last one should be no surprise. Sex, Self, and Surprise. Now this is the part all the men will enjoy, and when you start getting what you want, you will too. Give your man all the sex he can handle. If he wants it three times a day give it to him five times a day. Calm down, it not as hard as you make it to be. It could be a ten-minute session. Give him all the sex you can, until he just hardly wants it anymore. Lol. If you have children don't start complaining and making excuses, find a way! If you were trying to catch him in the beginning, you would. I have experienced many times when a woman has let me have some and when a woman has given me some. It's not the same, there is a difference. When a woman let's, a man has some it's alright. When a woman give's her man some, she gives herself to him. When a woman gives herself to a man, her body, mind and her emotions watch out now! Get involved! If you don't know you must learn how to give yourself to your man. Most women already know men are not as outgoing as them when it comes to their sexual expression. So, you need to be the one who initiates and creates spontaneous times and places. The key to surprise is initiate, initiate and initiate. After you have successfully completed all four phases consistently for 90 days there is nothing, he won't give you within his means. That means be practical if he can't afford it or not able to do it than you can't have it.

Let's briefly reflect on the important parts we discussed. Women be proud of being soft and delicate. Embrace your feminine and use your power. And remember you are designed by nature to want things and receive. So, the more you give him man language, quality time, acts of service, sex, self, and surprises you will continue to receive more, more and more.

"LOVE IS A CHOICE THAT CREATES FEELINGS, NOT FEELINGS THAT MAKES YOU CHOOSE." DC

This book is created from an account of how I experienced a time in my life. Were a woman knowing how to get along with a man. It is not normal in today's society for relationships to just work out without working it out. Most women are told even before their teenager to enjoy their singlehood focus on their career, spend money, travel and enjoy hanging out with their friends, before getting serious with a man. Many women are told not to focus on a man just their 5-year plan. This book is for the woman who choose to find her way back to her true femininity and self-love thru her expression of self. This type of journey is with the interaction with others showing yourself separate from a man. As men and women, we have an innate fundamental desire for connecting with one another by design.

My experience has awarded me the privilege to share with a woman in her natural state as she brought me to mine. I experienced a proud woman embracing her femininity her softness and kind nature. Always expressing her feminine energy thru her words, touch and environment. She didn't find her feminine nature in things but in her enter self. When she expressed, I made her feel safe and secure? She respected and accepted me. I made her comfortable and feel cherished. She was loyal and presented herself with kindness and grace among the public. Which made me want to carry myself to be responsible in my actions so she would have the emotional security she needed. And she regularly expressed acts of service to show her appreciation and need for me. While all the time never exchanging hurtful words or injuring one another's feeling. I would naturally give to her and give to her. This is when I knew a woman can get what she wants from a man.

Darrell Canty stands out with this surprising content with informative and impressionable information. This dynamic content provides the emotional and intellectual influence to engage this target audience. As an author he feels compelled to share this information with others. Expressing such joy and appreciation even if he never experiences a soulmate experience again. Many if not most people in their entire life will never experience one day of what he had for the most of nine years. Darrell Canty says, "he will be forever grateful and honored for the rest of his life."

The author can only hope to help one person find a true connection as he did. The time we spend here on earth means very little without an experience such as this. Once you have experienced this type of experience it will become a lifelong yearning. He can only imagine it to be like a drug attic experience that first high and forever chasing that high time and time again.

The author believes because of this experience he has become an author given a voice with something to say. I say thank you.

> "If a woman is giving a man everything but respect, she has given him nothing at all." Dc

Printed in the United States
by Baker & Taylor Publisher Services